CIRCULATION

KEN AUTREY

DOS MADRES

2023

DOS MADRES PRESS INC.
P.O. Box 294, Loveland, Ohio 45140
www.dosmadres.com   editor@dosmadres.com

Dos Madres is dedicated to the belief that the small press is essential to the vitality of contemporary literature as a carrier of the new voice, as well as the older, sometimes forgotten voices of the past. And in an ever more virtual world, to the creation of fine books pleasing to the eye and hand.

Dos Madres is named in honor of Vera Murphy and Libbie Hughes, the "Dos Madres" whose contributions have made this press possible.

Dos Madres Press, Inc. is an Ohio Not For Profit Corporation and a 501 (c) (3) qualified public charity. Contributions are tax deductible.

Executive Editor: Robert J. Murphy

Illustration & Book Design: Elizabeth H. Murphy
www.illusionstudios.net

Typeset in Adobe Garamond Pro & Bodoni Book
ISBN 978-1-953252-95-1
Library of Congress Control Number: 2023948208

First Edition

GRATITUDE

Heartfelt thanks to the Alabama State Council on the Arts for a fellowship that supported my efforts on this collection. My friends in The Deadline Club, though it disbanded years ago, remain an inspiration to me. More recently, my work has profited immeasurably from the guidance and good sense of those in our Poetry Salon. Over the years, I'm sure I have learned more from my students, young and old, than they have from me; their spirit has helped sustain my poetry. I am indebted to Hank Lazer for his guidance, friendship, and creative energy. And I deeply appreciate the editorial and design work of Robert and Elizabeth Murphy at Dos Madres Press.

*This book is for my sister Janice,
my wife Janne,
my daughters Nell and Tess,
and their families.*

.

TABLE OF CONTENTS

I.

II.

III.

IV.

CIRCULATION

I

The Invention of Time

Time is the moving image of eternity.
—Plato

In physics class, eleventh grade, I learned
how time was fiction and how long ago
around a sputtering fire someone happened
on the idea of dividing our lives
into seconds, minutes, years.
It didn't have to be this way,

claimed Mr. Guthrie, as he held a meter stick
to the blackboard and drew a white line
from one wall to the next.
"Imagine," his voice commanded,
"that line going on forever.
It does, you know, in our minds."

His rough hand rose to the board again
to draw a Jackson Pollock tangle of line
"There's nothing," the voice went on,
"to keep time from looking like that,
doubling in on itself, a maelstrom winding
berserk in three or four dimensions."

My mouth turned dry as chalk dust caught
in sunlight. I thought of afternoons
ticking away, the neat snapshots that punctuate
our days. I pondered the march of time,
that military trope evoking the thunder of boots, soldiers
in rigid rank, flags snapping in a steady breeze.

In fact, the army was a rag-tag band
of drunkards and pillagers, wandering
in a wilderness where trees had lost
their growth rings, seasons a figment
of some biologist's crazy urge
to have the colors change from time to time.

There is no time. You'll never see it, feel it,
hear it tromping by. Future and past are one.
I'm ageless, and I may grow young again.
my wristwatch is a joke,
as was that black-rimmed clock
that hung on the wall of our languid class.

When the bell sounded to end the period,
books slammed shut. Desks creaked.
Penny loafers, U.S. Keds and saddle shoes
clamored to the door and took us forward
through the ice age of the hall,
into the millennium of the streets.

Mnemonist

I am the man whose mind
will not forget, who calls forth
whole tableaus from all
the past, remembers every line
I've ever read. The days
reel back in photographic
density, each stippled sign
a gateway to bright stretches
that will not elude me.

One taste of apple bread
opens a sudden journey
into the sunlit kitchen
where my mother's elbows spread
like wings above quick clouds
of pastry flour. The way
her palms and fingers knead
the glowing dough reopens
galleries of painted peasants.

Unwittingly I see the staid
hands of Daumier's workers,
each stooping posture,
worn sleeve and nodding head
framed as it always will be
in my mind's unblinking gaze.
My ears know concerts played
ten years ago, each note
and rest a weary revelation.

This labyrinth, this travail
of exactitude, others envy
as they test my mastery
of names, dates, numbers, all
that keeps me from whatever
truths lie green and tangled
over this dogmatic wall
of fact. Even these words
now flatten into precision,
holding me in relentless thrall.

School Lunchroom

We filed in by class, handed sweaty quarters
to the girl tending the gray metal coin box.
In this domain of onion and candied yam,
we took what the hair-netted women ladled
onto our plates behind the steamy glass.
Always there were rolls, toasted and painted
lavishly with government surplus butter,
delicacy for which the word "sopping" was invented.

Late spring days, crowded at formica tables,
we plotted food fights, ten-year-old fingers itching
for greasy skirmish, a spoon of English peas catapulting
into the fifth grade section that would trigger all-out war:
gobs of mashed potato, clouds of mustard,
spurts of ketchup smearing the noon air.

We would eat only the golden rolls,
saving gravied Salisbury steaks and little wheels
of sliced tomato to sail across the lunchroom.
We would lob cartons of chocolate milk
like grenades, their spouts snapped open
to spew sweet arcs as they spun.

Even the principal, called when hostilities
broke out, would be powerless to restore order
in the face of such carnage. For this,
we could bear hunger into the afternoon.

But when Mrs. Mullins silently rose
from the teachers' table and walked her tray
to the conveyer belt, we followed
with our impeccable plates
and lined up alphabetically at the door,
a memory of butter glazing our lips.

Still Life with Piranhas

Billy O'Shea arced his hot dog
into the tank, and six of us watched
a flurry of fish become all teeth.
The knot untied as fast as it drew in,
and one pink shard of flesh remained
in the updraft. A silver flash
and even that was gone.
                                    We knew
how scrawny Brazilian cows blunder
into a cool river, linger a moment
too long and evaporate in a cloud
of flashing scales. Five minutes, then nothing
but bones. That mustard-soaked wiener
was closer to home and not much bigger,
really, than some kid's finger.
When the class gathered at the snow cone stand,
the teacher must have wondered why we slurped
so slowly.
                        And later, when nobody
banged on the Gila monster's glass
or rattled the monkey cages,
she figured the sun had sapped us.
That was several zoos ago. I can't recall
the teacher's name, and God knows how many
overheated cows have since been stripped
clean in the Amazon.
                                    Here I am lounging
in a wicker chair, engulfed by Sunday papers,
fingers smudged with news. They've arrested
a woman, 72, who neglected 112 chihuahuas

in her home. She seemed confused.
No statement yet from the SPCA.
My one good suit collects dust
in the closet, and the wingtips
go unpolished as I sort the facts.
This time I drop all pretense
of making them fit. I'm running
on faith.
                    You could say it's my religion,
this communion of piranha and chihuahua,
zoo and sunny den, finger and hot dog.
What should matter: whether the cops let her
change the threadbare robe or handcuffed her
in the squad car. And the question
of whom she called from the station.
What I remember: how the water's surface
never broke, the snow cone froze me to the bone,
and cherry syrup pooled in my flimsy cup.

Lighthouse

Glued to Howdy Doody, I thought Grandma was batty
to flick off the set and make Buffalo Bob
a spasm on the screen, his last vestige
a fading white dot.
In thunderstorms, she unplugged appliances,
feared the TV would explode,
pepper the room with shards of hot glass
if a random bolt shivered the antenna,
its crooked fork a stark invitation.

Now I know the stories of melted toasters,
and ruined microwaves. Better to live
in the dark a while. Or squander the light:
the way my wife leaves the set humming all night
when I'm away and no rough weather's forecast,
muffled talk one comfort of dreams.
She glides the hall when dawn breaks,
a cathode glow, the house intact
around a neat rectangle of static.

I heard a broadcast about a man
who made a mirror that shows the way
you really are, not reversed. He feels
it makes a difference, gives you a new glow.
But mirrors wouldn't lie.
Nor would Grandma, thinking safety
when the winds kicked up. Nor a lone wife,
my wife, who patrols the house before bed,
restless, flicking things on, electric comfort.

Meanwhile, I'm in the Star Motel,
talk show turned down low,
TV's locked beam choosing me
in the otherwise dark. An old woman enters
the set, hugs the host, and sits to chat.
I could turn the volume up,
but the sheets press on my chest.
Outside, the sky's starry.
Clear weather's supposed to hold.

The Explosion of the Kopper Kettle

The Kopper Kettle was the closest
you could get to fast food in our town.
The burgers, 12 cents apiece,
started as thin squares separated
with wax paper. Red-headed Sally
would peel one off and drop it
onto the grill where it puckered
and cooked in two minutes.
She served it on a square bun
with a dollop of shredded onion.

The Kopper Kettle exploded
early one Sunday morning
due to a leaky gas line
that somehow caught a spark.
The explosion blew out
church windows a block away
but miraculously came
too early for the Methodist crowd,
and not a soul was injured.
The eatery was a total loss.

Despite our prayers, it was razed
and replaced by an insurance office.
People still talk about those delicacies,
how you could eat four or five
with no problem and then come back
for more the next day. Those few
who witnessed the big bang tell how
little squares of beef, thawed
and sizzled by the blast, came down
like manna all over town.

Hilyer's Junkyard

It was a shabby outpost between Auburn
and Opelika, sprawling aside a clear stretch
of road in the days before strip malls
and fastfood joints stitched the two towns
together. Back then, Hilyer's seemed remote
from any civilized settlement, although
it bloomed with stretches of wreckage jettisoned
from those very towns that kept their distance.
Driving past, you could hardly tell house
and office from the axle heaps, castoff stoves,
spent air conditioners, head-high snarls of pipe,
and Rorschachs of twisted metal
from the mill a few miles away.

My classmate Charlie Hilyer saw no shame
in such squalor. What boy would turn his back
on a life played out in an eternity of auto carcasses.
He came to school without homework
but with pockets full of cogs and bolts
salvaged from the lush wastage of his back yard.
One day he wore a grease-smeared
bandage on one hand. The day before,
a pipe bomb had sheared off a finger.
The men in his clan were connoisseurs
of missing parts. Even his cousin Wayne
had a glass eye, eerie talisman
from a BB gun accident.

Clad in overalls, Charlie's huge father
seldom budged from his chair
beside the office door, country music radio
an arm's length away. The men in town
knew where to go for a spare hinge or hubcap.
He'd tell them right where to look,
how much to pay, inventory and account book
locked in his head. In my rare visits,
that country of rust and grime, necessary
and strange, gripped me like no Saturday matinee.
Leaving, riding shotgun in my father's Dodge,
I'd ponder, not quite death, but all
we left behind and couldn't ever know.

Rope Lesson

I sit in a clump of Boy Scouts after Hobo Stew
hearing fire lick, watching my dad tie knots
beneath the stars: bowline and sheet bend,
half hitch and square. His fingers conjure hanks
into shapes that hold while there's pressure.
Keep it tight, he says, and your pack will never shift,
your sail's boom never slip.

Rope's part thread, part muscle. I follow it
forward and back, feel its texture.
I fumble with a hank of sisal, snarling it,
snipping more, trying a sheep shank. One moment
I add oak chunks to a faltering fire, watch flames
twist like tempered hemp. The next, my fingers
tend strands I'll pull into cat's cradle, teacup.

Rope is a message of lines.
Bend it, twist it, but it stops
in a sharp cut, a nub, a snarl. Weave strands back,
and the end's blunt as a billy club.
Fire is radiant, circular. It moves up and out.
It goes on, showering sparks, growing smoke.
Fire exaggerates our shadows.

I watch his hands against an olive shirt.
This is how I know him.
This is how I know you.
We all have knots to tie and untie.
You sit at a wavering fire with others.
Your mind is on your father,
his syllables, tricks, and coils.
It's dark, you hear words, and you follow.

In Medias Res

In Brazil my father cut a hole
in a dairy cow's side and installed a porthole
that could be removed like the lid of a jar
so his grad students could study
bovine digestion *in medias res*,
or "in the middle of things,"
as Horace put it in *The Art of Poetry*.

In storytelling, the critic thought,
this was preferable to *ab ovo*,
beginning at the beginning,
literally "of the egg," as when
Helen hatched from Leda's egg.

The research on cattle, which Dad left
in the middle of Brazil, led to
improved cattle nutrition and milk production
in Minas Gerais, a name meaning
"general mines," although the ore
was long since taken from its middle.

We all begin *ab ovo*, but we interrupt
our parents' lives. They die midway
through our own stories, leaving us
to puzzle over the mystery
of their beginnings just as we wonder
about our death, about which we know
only that it will come *in medias res*.

What I Thought I Knew

After the long wait for Dad's death,
the pouring out of words, then
ten years later, Mom's quiet departure,
and more lines and stanzas
honed for solace, I thought I had little
more to say about those days,
the tying and untying of knots
that mark our lives as children.
But now, waking each morning
in this house I find, not exactly
their ghosts or shadowy echoes
in the halls, nothing
so common. Instead, I see
their indelible fingerprints
on the faucets, page corners
in their books turned down,
old shoe scuffs in the room
where now my slippers whisper.
So, part of aging, this house
tells me, is to find that never
does the need to reimagine
what I thought I knew die out.

Shotguns

It seemed he was taken from us
without warning in the night,
contents of his pockets emptied
and strewn after a day's work.
In fact, it was a long, slow fade:
Alzheimer's, a stroke, the hospital.
Words faltered on his lips for months.

Shotgun shells littered his dresser.
Also, a pile of coins,
two rumpled handkerchiefs,
an unprocessed roll of film.
One day Mom asked
can't you do something
with those shells? And you know
the guns are still in the closet.

I dumped the ammo into a paper bag,
took the 20-gauge and the narrow-barreled
410 from behind his old shoes,
checking, as he always taught me,
to make sure they weren't loaded.
At home, I propped them
in my own closet and stuck the shells
at the back of my sock drawer.

As for the film, the prints came back blurry
And washed-out along with a message:
Prompt development may prevent
deterioration in print quality.

Dim forms haunt the ruined surfaces.
I keep the photos like a deck of cards
on my dresser. Dad always said
you have to play the hand you're dealt.

Elegy for My Father

The words of my father's life
froze in my grasp last winter.
They would not thaw.
I carried them months, and then
one April day, I placed them on a shelf
beside the tattered wallet
he carried on his hip.
The words have risen into the air
and at times fall to my tongue
like bright mints, the ones
in a small roll on his dresser.
These are not the words
that fill old hymns to the dead:
no "anguish" or "regret" among them.

Summer evenings a raspy chorus of locusts
rises and falls in the heat,
and the word "cicada" comes to me,
bringing on its wings a glimpse of my father
holding a papery insect shell in his palm.
The word "rope" appears,
and in its simple syllable
I find him mooring a boat,
securing a pack frame,
hanging a swing in the back yard.

One morning, just when I fear
the language of my father has faded
like the ink of his wartime letters,
I pour myself a mug of coffee,
hear in his voice the word "java,"
and feel in my hands a warmth
that endures all day.

Mints

A child slung from the hip
or a smudged arm often tugged Mother
off center or coaxed her out of the frame.
In this shot she gingerly supports
my leg in a cast, broken as I took my first steps.
The overexposed white plaster draws
the light, leaving her face in shadow.

Here, she is half concealed by the shoulder
of my father, his string of fish,
his nub of cigar. I had thought
he smoked only when driving late
and wasn't one to gloat over the day's catch.
Is it really him on that Florida wharf?
I feel him edging his wife out again—
though she was always the talker.

In this one she appears in a Halloween gypsy get-up—
out of character, wordless, dark eye-liner—
grinning by the front door. I'm in my father's shoes
as he presses back against the flowered wallpaper
to catch the sequined blouse's full effect,
the scarf at her waist. My eye follows his
through the lens of the camera he bought
in the Philippines just after the war and loves
to sling from his shoulder like an ammo pouch.

Her quick fade from view comes with practice.
If she stays too long away from the circle
of molten candy on white marble,

no amount of pulling can save it:
the sinewy strands will crumble into sugar.
Timing is the secret of the creamy mints
which scent the house for hours after
the pleasing snap of that sweet rope
she twists then snips apart. See how
my father and I sit at the kitchen table
as the pale green nuggets melt
and melt on our speechless tongues.

Gravity

1.

To my mother, now bedridden, a moored vessel,
travel was mere skittering across the surface.
Instead, she wanted to set up housekeeping, settle in.

Wherever she went—Colombia, Brazil—she packed along
her sewing projects, her ease in baking rolls or chicken.
Now she cannot walk, much less venture onto the *llanos*.

Her stories have been cast off—or locked inside.
Now I have the power of the word. She needs me.
Occasionally her good right hand reaches

across her placid body to the left arm, inert
on its pillow, to rub or reposition it, coax it
back into action. It's the most she can do.

Early on, we harbor the fear that someone listens,
and then, the fear that no one does. As I pack for Italy,
my mother says she's glad she doesn't have to go.

The great dark outside blankets all of us, outlasts
even the ravages of sunlight, said to be stunning
in Rome. Her voice grows faint over the phone.

2.

She never gets out of bed.
Her lifeless left side

keeps her there at the mercy
of her daughter and her nurse,
providers of food, drink,
cleanliness, fresh bedclothes.

But this one afternoon
she stirs and seems to hover
in the air, suspended,
as a parade of visitors
comes bearing cards
and good wishes: for comfort?
a long life? the year ahead?
She asks, "Aren't we lucky?"

I photograph the guests
entering in clusters. She never tires
of posing with them,
her good right side smiling
to spite her passive left.
For once, her appetite is enormous.

3.

My mother grips the bed rail, clings
to a life raft. Covers ripple and surge
like waves. She slowly sinks
into the gulf that gapes beneath us all,
depths that beckon us with a name
we've never heard before. Her face
pales against the gravity, same
today as yesterday, of a stark refrain,
the ancient tide-worn jinx.

Her left arm rests aboard a pillow,
hovers like driftwood in slight current.
Hair, freshly combed, spills up
like splayed seaweed.
Those ruined legs, lumps beneath
the sheets, once kicked her across
a mile of rough water in the teeth
of a churning wind, rowboat
in her wake, acres of fish below.

Time's all, or nothing, to her now.
She sends out signals, not quite
sentences, but flares from the bow.
I look in and find her wide-eyed,
a gaze part wonder, part fear.
She's not sure what she's after—
other than the need to have me near.
I whisper low the lifeguard's mantra:
first reach or throw, next row, then go.

Hunger

The apple plays its old part
well, oval heart sudden
in its subtle throb, seeded
like that fruit, deep, forbidden,

offered sparingly to those
who choose to take it gently
in their hands but leave it whole,
in need of feeling saintly.

Eve's luscious morsel
cannot fail to disappoint
all who would test its sweetness,
and confess a need to bite,

while those who trouble the heart,
dare start in careful haste,
spend no time on regret,
endure no waiting and are blessed.

Ménage à Trois

Darkness falls on the interstate,
as two pairs of feet
break my white-line trance,
jut at me from a flatbed truck
just ahead, a couple
rapt in one another,
doing seventy
beneath a sleeping bag
that flaps in the breeze
like a tattered wing.

Together on the truck's boards
in lover's limbo, oblivious
to the danger of rolling
off beyond speed limits,
milestones, billboards,
and the prying eyes of strangers,
the two whose age I can't discern
lie where shrill wind
and the traffic's drone
frame them, where gritty pavement
sounds a muffled undertone.

The driver, hat dipping low,
must have business down the road.
I roar past the entangled cargo
and find his vision locked ahead
even when I try to catch his eye.
Behind him, behind us both, they follow
the call of another road,
where warmth is mere suggestion,
love the only true direction.

Mask

I put on a mask and fell in love.
She stared at the mask and swore
I should never change. Alone,
I pulled off my mask and didn't know
myself. The mirror showed me the man
I had left behind. When I again placed
the mask on my face, my eyes clouded,
but when I next saw her, the air
turned crystalline. Slowly the mask
grew to fit me, or my features changed
to match its contours. I learned
to keep it in place even when she was
far away. In rare moments when I slid
the mask off, I gazed at it with dismay.
One day when the mask had almost
become a part of me, I peeled it off
and held it out to her. She took it gingerly,
a wrinkle in her brow. Slowly, she removed
her own mask, gave it to me, and lifted
my mask to her face. When her mask
rested on my face, it fit perfectly.
Our eyes met, and we saw one another
as though for the first time.

Pilgrims

Pretend the phone call
never got beyond a tangle of wires
inside some windowless brick building
where there are no human places.
Pretend the light you cannot snap off
in your head begins to waver,
affected by some distant storm,
then collapses to a glow,
faint and manageable.
Imagine all noises overhead
as just loose shingles
on the roof, or harmless
scrabbling of mice in an attic.

Near Bogota, behind a vast cathedral
on some town's tallest hill,
I saw a building squat and nondescript.
Inside—no furniture,
only four walls laden
with relics of the healed:
scrawled ecstatic prayers
nailed up with newly muscled
hands, renderings of Christ,
and in one corner
a forest of cast-off crutches.

Imagine pinned among the rabble
of notes in a language
you and I cannot read,
the mountaintop photograph
I took of you. Pilgrims, unsure
what brought you here, rub gently
your sunburned face.

The Ice Skaters

Inside our corner house of hewn timber
and clapboard, we sleep late, quilts piled
like snow, and warmly hear the rattling wind.
A sliver of day wakes us, as the cat
paws the bedroom door. Outside—winter's old
subterfuge: bright drifts appearing
to coat the world in truth
expose the bone of hill, the broken barn,
the apple tree's ungainly limbs.
The pasture pond, cupped and frozen,
gleams with new-carved light, no longer
hidden in a barricade of rushes.

Later we hike down with skates slung
from our shoulders, aiming to try
the seasonal balancing act again.
Our shovels scrape the surface free
of snow, and through an oval rink,
the water's veiny blue seeps up.
Beneath our wobbling blades
and summer ankles, the new ice
holds as we build speed and lift,
gripping hands, until—
remote as figures out of Bruegel—
we warm again to one another
in lineaments of glazed grace.
The sudden heart's command, oblivious
and sure, sustains us as we glide
above forgotten fish, under
a white and looming sky.

Point Savory

The day being gone, I took
in the living room, the way
the sun nudged the Moroccan carpet
before leaving to haunt the bay,

then the island, its scrawny palms,
and soon, the far side of the globe.
That was the evening I left off
the lamps, letting the dark throb

in its own good time.
It happened quickly. One
minute I scanned the news
headlines in my lap. Then

I held only a blur of gray.
If you surrender to the night,
it pulls back. The amber wine
ripples with shards of light.

Candles recall their flicker.
Imperfect dark cannot sustain
its bleakness. We see through it
just as it conspires to end

our daily sojourn. The spare
and lonesome glow of the moon,
even when a sliver, stretches
stubborn day into the gloom.

Intoxiphilia

Don't ever drink alone,
I've always heard, but
the two or three fingers
of scotch tinting the ice that clinks
as I tilt the glass thrill me, a little
Titanic of gusto after the late news.
And then one more dollop
as the cubes shrink and my wife
slips into sleep a floor above.
Through the windows the night
surrounds us like the deepest brew.
Before the stairs lead me up
to her warmth, the whiskey
chills. Hours ahead of me,
the coffee's set to murmur and waft
in the kitchen when she descends
at daybreak. Once in bed, I forget
the single malt, and turn
my dreams toward the cupped
darkness that will lift us
together into morning light.

Rubbings

I reach out in small night hours
to touch those hands that years
ago played across gravestones
on a hill in Marblehead.

We were young and held death
at arm's length as we unrolled sheets
of paper, taping them to upright slabs,
grainy and chipped in the salt air.

With dark crayons we rubbed over
chiseled surfaces, watching
names and dates emerge
from lichen shadows.

We peeled away winged skulls,
cherubs, worn rosettes,
and words once made
by hands as young as ours.

I can almost see you crouched
in those years before children,
coaxing lines from granite
in dark swirls—the epitaphs

rose quickly to your fingertips
while I knelt to steady the paper
or stood away in sunlight, watching
how you leaned into your work.

Afterwards, eating sandwiches and fruit,
we read the plodding verses, set them aside,
and gazed over the arc of ocean
beyond the tethered yachts.

Now I reach for you in darkness,
yearning to defy death and wait
for words to work up through
the old stones of memory.

The Vigil

My heart beats like a prison drum at dawn.
We stand again in the prow of a small ship.
The waters lap against the face of Eden,
and all the broken histories fall around us.

We stand again in the prow of a small ship
so small it's little more than just a wish,
and all the broken histories fall around us
until the safety of a secret port.

So small it's little more than just a wish,
my watch will shatter in the sunlight.
Until the safety of a secret port
our travels haunt the deep meridian.

My watch will shatter in the sunlight
and coax away forgotten serenades.
Our travels haunt the old meridian
between the garden and the grave.

To coax away forgotten serenades
I slip into the rhythm of the islands
between the garden and the grave.
The two of us believe these walls will tremble

and slip into the rhythm of the islands.
As waters lap against the face of Eden,
We know all human walls rise up to tremble.
My heart beats like a prison drum at dawn.

Home Port

Lying in bed disheveled
beneath ripples of quilt,
she asks if I had dreams.
Some figment winging
like a hawk through fog,
distant and peripheral,
tells me I did. I drift back
into the voyage.

I remember the Merlot
sipped last night, its tang
and luster. The final lines
in the book I closed
at eleven-thirty still hover
at my shoulder. But what came
next under the moon's transit
remains as dark as a freighter's hold.

Bright-eyed, she reclines
in blind-slatted light,
head on a cocked elbow,
reliving the carnival of her sleep—
babbling friends and strangers,
creatures that prowled her Amazons,
the careening autos and planes she rode
through a wilderness of road and sky.

Woozy at her side, I watch
the murky film noir
I've just escaped fade

into seaside pastels, then hues
of the late Van Gogh. I place
my feet on morning's shore.
Day looms at the window
like a sunflower ripe for picking.

Enclosure

1.

The heart's dark basket throbs
coil upon coil, reeds woven
like veins of water
through an Asian delta

or over animal trails
on the African savannah.
Its strands bend without
snapping, surge without

bursting through all days
but the worst, reason
for hope even in bleak
moments beyond midnight.

2.

Within, a box, fashioned
of blood-dark wood
yawns silently, its top
inlaid with squares,

an Indian chessboard
whose pieces long since
made their break
from the heart's prison.

No one knows why
the box goes on
opening and closing
like a hungry mouth.

3.

Its companion, a cylinder
fashioned of cinnamon, carved
with ancient letters, goes on
throbbing, sweet cargo

sent round the body's world.
This chamber too
is hard to crack,
nor would we want to.

But this is the one always
coaxing us into the world,
urging us through the Amazons
of our fears and lusts.

4.

Then there's a third, forgotten
in the spiking of all
the machines, in the beating
of each coiled mystery.

This is the one we live for,
the antechamber thriving
even in our woe, our agony,
the hopeful muscle

that no stethoscope fathoms,
no echocardiogram detects.
It defies logic and awakens only
to the whisper of another heart.

Sahel

Some poems have to survive
without water. Let the few syllables
from these parched lips
come to rest like pebbles
rolling unprovoked
into an Arabian gulch.
Rhythms of fish and lapping wave
have no place here. Ponds, pools,
and shaded streams turn
into roadmaps of unreadable cracks.
Bamboo and fern shrink to cactus,
with its harsh burst of yellow flower.
Only hissing windblown sand,
the scrabble of lizard feet, or
a boulder's crude settlement
disturb this buzzard silence.

There is no way this poem will echo
fish crows on my father's lake,
taste of fresh tomatoes
dipped in ocean brine, display
the mallard's deep green head,
or catch the moist scents rising
from newly planted herbs.
English thyme, Corsican mint, oregano,
tricolor sage, globe basil, rosemary:
none of these are meant to taint
these lines. Instead, I think
of your smooth shoulders, strong
as driftwood bleached in sun.
And I see again the deep, dry eyes
of a stone Buddha staring out
at us across all that open space.

Christmas Cards

How do they do it? These families
that send out slick group photos,
all eyes open, every child beaming.
Each year we swear we too will plan
a winning tableau, three generations
decked out and color coordinated,
arrayed on a sunny beach, smiling,
a little windblown—or the twelve of us
alert and casual on the front steps
of our neat, spacious home,
wreathed door as a backdrop.

But when we assemble for the camera,
one child whines and wants to climb
out of the picture. Someone is missing
the white shirt and khaki pants.
Or we wait too late in the day,
and we're all hungry, looking like
sullen savages intent on the next kill.
Even the time we gave the kids candy
as a bribe, two of them ate it on the spot,
and only later did we detect chocolate
smears marring their broad smiles.

Now it's time to order this year's card,
and we have not one group portrait to prove
we're perfect, nothing to show for
twelve months of warmth and unity.
Instead, we'll fall back on a lame collage
of faces, mugs captured here and there,

assembled five-by-seven and sent out
over "Happy Holidays" to all those
contented families sipping cider around
an impeccable tree, lights aglow
and not a single bulb burned out.

Expedition

When kids are sick they'll put up with this,
so we nestle them on the carpet,
darken the room, and another slide
drops into the projector. As they feed
languidly, popcorn scatters like snow
on a spruce tree in Elmira.
Deserts like this one, Sonora, mid-July,
are hot enough to melt a camera.
On the Serengeti a wildebeest herd,
river of hoof and fur, migrates
for hours across the road.
We inch through in a Land Rover.

Across the room, my daughter's royal python
basks under fluorescent light in the tank
we bought for fish and then sublet
to gerbils. A fraction of his mature length,
sometimes he curls in her palm, woozy
with human warmth. The family itself
is pacified as the projector hums.
Here's the rail of a ship underway.
Miami's skyline slowly shrinks,
as in those gradual moments up the coast
at Cape Canaveral when, ignited,
a rocket inches off the pad.

The guide points to a huge tank.
At liftoff three hundred thousand
gallons of water flood the flame trench,
to absorb the heat that launches a payload.

Shipboard, the calypso band plays "Sail Away."
Land hazes over, palm trees now toylike.
Sunbathers preen in deck chairs,
The boat churns the sea's deep blue
into a green of new leaves.
Another slide, and the shuttle drops
its fuel tanks, rotates in silence,
a gold blur out where there is no music.

The girls orbit into sleep. I click off
the projector light and keep the fan on
a minute to cool the bulb. The python
stretches. In the night's wake
the past sheds its skin.

Trick

Bags rustling with loot,
far afield in the neighborhood,
at last my daughters turn back.
I have shadowed them, watching
the soft knock at each door,
their unkempt costumes,
handouts from safe porches,
stuffed sheets dangling
from trees. Voices hardly their own
muffle through dime store masks.
I am a vampire, a sucker
for the dark. They merge
like conspirators in the arc
of a streetlight
then sprint up our driveway,
everything but candy
out of their minds.

I creep through the back door
as wrapped sweets cascade
onto the Oriental rug.
The annual rule here: all candy
must be eaten in one night—
no lingering stashes of toffee or kisses.
They see the orgy of consumption
as a blessing, a required binge.
They claw first into all chocolate,
then the chewier stuff,
saving sour nuggets for last.
In a while they've had enough,

untouched candy and spent wrappers
a cloying harvest.
They leave, capes and robes peeled off,
strewn like husks. I am alone now,
in from the woods, scavenging
what my daughters have left behind.

My Daughter Rowing

After supper, scant light left
in the day, my daughter is rowing
on the lake. Mountain air stirs,
and I watch from the shore.
Sleeveless, jeans rolled,
shoes left on the dock,
she pulls into light wind,
gaze unfolding on her wake.

In the Andes, the Aymara
imagine the future hidden at their backs,
the past ahead in view. My daughter too
watches the past go out in ripples
before her. Almost muscular arms
roll the oars in brass locks.

Twelve months ago,
on our last visit
to the lake, she struggled
with this craft.
Years ago, one voyage,
I dressed her warmly,
propped her in the stern,
and took her to the island. Then,
she had only to lie back, testing
chilly water with her fingers.

Suddenly, my daughter is ashore,
shaking her hair, leaving the lake
without a backward glance.
Early tomorrow we return
home, to the future
that widens behind us.

On My 52nd Birthday

I had always thought of the present as morning—as prologue.
Now I realized that for me, at least, it is not. It is afternoon—
the afternoon of a day that will bring nothing more than the
fatigue and, perhaps, the peace of the evening.
                                        —George Kennan, at age 52

I slip into the afternoon of my life
leaving the door ajar behind me as though
I could decide to turn back.
Morning grows quaint. These bifocal eyes
absorb the later light, shadows
under old oaks, ivy sprawling.

Starting fresh every day, looking
to a peaceful evening, I find
the door hinge, oiled with memory,
swivels well, a riddle of passage.

Last week a waitress gave me
the Senior Citizen's discount
for a cup of coffee.
This morning I was distracted by a list
of the world's 100 best movies.

My mother calls, reminds me: 52 years ago
in Pennsylvania coal country, I was born
a week late with long fingernails,
scratches on my fat red face.
She says my father, now confined to the house,
has lost his love of beautiful wood.

My daughter, just out of college,
prepares quiche for my birthday.
My wife vacuums the living room rug.
For now, those I love seem safe.

In day's waning warmth, I come under
the spell of meandering talk
and good music, embrace evening
with full and heavy heart.

Before the Wedding

My daughter sits
in a silk robe beside
the bedroom window.

Her hair is impeccable,
fixed in a bun the veil
will soon cover.

She is passive,
hands at rest
on her crossed legs.

She says little
as attendants
move around her

like courtesans,
powdering her face,
preparing her gown.

For long moments
she stares out the window
at the overcast sky.

A slight wind troubles
late spring leaves.
She waits until the last

possible minute to rise
and begin to dress.
At the flourishing

of crinoline and lace,
I leave the room,
closing the door

on a cluster of women
sipping champagne.
As I walk downstairs

their voices blur
like the murmur
of nesting birds at dusk.

Talking to My Granddaughter

I tell her the best stories I know
as she squirms in my lap,
starfish hands reaching up
for my glasses. This is the way
I imagine my grandfathers
talked to me in the year before
I stumbled onto my first word.
As she fashions her own truth
I want to give her all I know.

Her pink skin is faultless,
creased at wrist, elbow,
and knee, puppet-like, and I play
the ventriloquist, planting words
in her mouth to take root in time.
I want language as lucid as her skin,
fresh as the scent of her tufted scalp.
Like a cat, she makes no mistakes.
She is true to herself, her baby-ness.

Into the tiny question marks
of her ears falls this merger
of vowel and consonant
we name speech.
In time she will hold forth
herself, weave her own text
of the world. What I tell her
will fade into mere syllables,
faint memories of oooh and aaah
uttered in the innocence of old age.

Turtle

Just when I think my school days
are finally behind me, faded and lost
in the chalk dust of my sixties,
I watch my first-grade granddaughter
bend over the dining room table
with her page of homework
painstakingly coaxing the word
"turtle" out of a pencil that totters
in her grasp. Her left hand splays
on the page, holding it in place.

The paper looks the same
as what I used in Miss Duggar's
class fifty-six years ago: off-white
with light blue lines an inch apart
and dotted lines in between
to help me know where to cross
the "t" or confine the small "u."

Her tongue juts through the gap
from her missing front teeth
as she prints the angles and curves
that will give her one word,
then two, and eventually,
after endless erasures and
reams of marred paper,
the whole world.

As she completes the "e,"
she relaxes, takes a deep breath,
and leans back to survey her work,
just as I do when, after decades
of fits and starts, I reach the end
of a hard-won poem.

Electricity

Just east of Pascagoula, The Gator Ranch sign
blares, "Take a Walk on the Wild Side,"
its red arrow pointing down a gravel track
off Highway 90, where a machine
with giant whirling blades has lopped off
branches of pine trees lining the shoulder,
limbs torn as though by some huge beast.
In the back seat, my granddaughter fidgets
for swamp life, and when I park
in front of the garish pink gift shop, I see
the spread is in fact more swamp than ranch.

We get tickets and stroll on the boardwalk
to inspect the snouted reptiles in a fenced,
algae-covered pond. I buy a bag
of food pellets. Wired, she tosses them
toward the mouths that surge
and snap when morsels pepper
the murky water. We board an airboat,
careen and swirl through the swamp,
slowing to see creatures crouched placid
in the gloom of palmettos. The driver
jolts them into action with marshmallows.

Later, a man hands my granddaughter
a baby gator, jaws bound
with a rubber band, tail ticking
back and forth. In the shop we find
t-shirts, stuffed animals, plastic snakes,
shot glasses, postcards, and in one corner,

an electric chair, relic from the old prison,
arm and leg straps hanging like tongues
from timeworn wood. I stop her
just as she veers over to sit in it,
hold her close, and feel her shudder
as we choose ice cream bars
from the humming freezer by the door.

No Certain Claim

The restless waiting holds me like a spell.
My daughter's son will take my father's name.
Which door will open? None of us can tell.

The summer's long demise, its ghostly knell
sounds out, and nothing ever stays the same.
The eager waiting holds me like a spell.

Some days I pass like heaven's infidel,
a silent wanderer, no certain claim.
Which door will open? None of us can tell.

I hear my mother's voice, clear as a bell,
call out to me, her world a shrinking frame.
The awful waiting holds me like a spell.

Grandchild and parent, each within a cell,
seek out the key to this confining game.
Which door will open? None of us can tell.

These lonely vigils: who can stand them well?
I keep my peace and feed the earthly flame.
The endless waiting holds me like a spell
Which door will open? None of us can tell.

Eclipse

At the moment of totality, you know
where you are. Weeks ago
you bought the black glasses
that would make the sun safe,
allow you to study the moon's
dark chasm ringed by a thin corona.
We are always after totality, aren't we,
one moment locking together night and day,
vacancy of the new moon, glow
of the old sun, mirror twins,
one a match for the other
in the innocent globes of our eyes?
Recall the craze of 3-D movies,
crowds gazing at screens like hordes
of blank-eyed zombies. You sat and waited
for the spear to catch you between the eyes,
the burning car to roll into your lap.
Can anyone recall the stars?
On the crowded lawn, it's no
picture show when for once the moon
plays itself, not a mere reflection.
In time, the glasses come off,
and we rub our eyes as the vagrant
cameo steals away and disappears,
returning as a wiser ghost at midnight,
borrowing muted white from the star
it black-balled in the alien afternoon.

Heat Wave

South of Scranton, going seventy
toward Harrisburg, I come upon gray mounds
of slag from the mines. Around a curve—
acres of battered cars. Sun rays pound
the wreckage. I was born in the valley
below this chrome and steel graveyard.
Under some of these hills, coal
fires have smoldered thirty years.

Ten miles away my nearly blind uncle works
crossword puzzles through a magnifying glass.
Lungs shot, he doesn't get out much.
My aunt, overweight, in love with ice cream,
teaches piano lessons in a small front room.
When trains cross Pringle Street,
the roar drowns out all music.

Summer visits, I'd walk out to savor
pretzel factory smells, returning
with black dust in the crease of each arm.
Now, trucks never whine through neighborhoods.
to send coal clattering down cellar chutes.

The Susquehanna flooded a decade ago.
No one believed the river would reach
the second story. Water pulled family
albums from a closet shelf. Photos floated off
with sheet music and the dining room set.
In one lost shot I was four, swallowed
by a winter coat, standing between snow drifts,
a fender of my uncle's Ford visible.

As I speed past a runaway
truck ramp, a rockslide barely misses me.
I count my blessings in the next bar,
the Anthracite Inn, drinking to my aunt
and uncle who never touch a drop.
The bartender sets out tiny pretzels
shaped like a beer company logo.
Flood photos line a wall. Outside,
my sleeves are coated with dust. The earth
warms up. Afternoon unfolds in black and white,
a crossword puzzle without a clue.

Reading Dante on Eagle Crag Lake

The light was departing. The brown air drew down
all the earth's creatures, calling them to rest
from their day-roving, as I, one man alone,

prepared myself to face the double war
of the journey and the pity, which memory
shall here set down, nor hesitate, nor err.

—Dante, *The Inferno*, Canto II, trans. John Ciardi

THE JOURNEY

Placing coins on toll road tongues, I cross
into July, skirt the snarl of Manhattan,
follow the Hudson to its source on the flank
of the Adirondacks, then veer west forty miles
to Conifer Road, which leads to a timber town,
now a few streets of slumped houses
surrounded by balsams and hemlocks,
a shrinking settlement left
from when the sawmill spit out lumber.
Southward a potholed road takes me
past Mt. Arab and its fire tower.
Arriving at the lake at dusk, I hear loons;
each year a raucous couple flies north
to this summer home.
I carry groceries and duffle bags down
the trail to the brown cabin, third structure
built on the mile-long lake. Logs
from the twenties record provisions
hunters brought and the deer they killed.
Three years since my last visit, I
walk the ninety-year-old path

past the outhouse, the woodshed,
the well, to the four-room camp
built with lumber brought in by rail
and carried two hundred yards
to the lakeside. Before stowing
gear to last six weeks, I stride to the dock,
squint at the crags to the southwest,
scan for the cruising loons.

THE PITY

We bring our burdens to these shores,
measuring ourselves against
the hunters and lumberjacks
who came in the twenties
and before that the Algonquins
who roamed the woods, leaving
no remnant of their passage.
A photo tacked to the wall shows the hill
across the lake ravaged by fire,
its slopes a scattering of black
timbers. The land, so forgiving,
has long since buried its own ashes.
A photo tucked between pages
of the hunters' log shows them
bunched unshaven at the potbelly,
suspenders and whiskey
holding them together,
a deck of cards askew on a table.
Across the lake the late sun ignites
the crags—remote, otherworldly,

outcrop chunks of granite
planted deep and overlooking
a lake born before history began.

MEMORY

The woods hide traces not just
of forbears but of my own past,
paltry now in the waning. I say
I come each year for renewal.
The long days take me back
to old myths. The lake, clear
and deep, some days gives up
its mysteries: bass cruising
the shallows, crayfish scuttling
from boulder to boulder, minnows
flaring as they catch the light.
Other days it's a mirror,
sending back nothing more
than what hangs above it:
sky, cloud, distant osprey,
one querulous face
in search of its own Beatrice.

Air and Water

Lying on a Vermont dock growing old,
I soak up the western sun
before easing into a lake so cold
that even unseasonable highs
can't warm its glacial waters.
One foot, then another, then knees,
thighs, and groin, feel the chill
rise from rocky shallows
that refract everything, allow
a clear view of the bottom
while wrenching every limb askew,
trick mirror with ripples
that blur the magic.

When my body's in
all the way I'm guillotined
on a July afternoon, torso frozen
senseless, disembodied,
lips quivering, eyes wide with panic,
head afloat as though there's nothing
below. But then, buoyed
by my blood's wild resurgence,
a shiver of submarine warmth,
I take heart and duck,
reveling in the world each man
was made from but not destined for.

Could this be a glimpse of how
we end, head propped above
rippling sheets and then in a moment

covered, shackled to a worthless body?
Or might this instant bring a plunging
resurrection, feet, hands, and eyes
reclaimed in the depths of their origins,
as we swim breathless
with all the old beasts?

Kayak

Let me not fall back on the word
"knife" to tell you how my kayak
parted the morning waters, nor "dip"
to capture the rhythmic immersion
of my paddle. The lake was not smooth
as glass, nor was it a lake.

No hickory smoke permeated
the air, and although my wife tended
the cabin, no coffee awaited me
to wash down buttery pancakes
turned out of an iron skillet
and slathered in syrup.

Pancakes, in fact, were no more
available than dancing coyotes,
though there was a distant howl
at midnight that startled us
awake as we lay quilted
on the screen porch.

I neither slept like the dead
nor caught forty winks
before the sun peeked above
the water's distant horizon.
Instead, the pines lining the road
obscured the sun.

It rose behind us as we gazed west
at the gray reservoir, gray monotony
lapping its breakfast at the shore.
Only then did I rouse myself,
pad down the trail to the dock,
slide the kayak into the shallows,

and ease into it carving a course
to the far side of Horseshoe Island,
and back past the west shore
where surging waves take
their toll, eroding the banks
to sheer pebble-embedded cliffs.

It's a whittling away to essentials
out here. No matter what anyone says,
it all amounts to fire,
water, sunlight, gloom,
rudimentary tools, and hunger
that floats in a storm.

The Wait

Fish veer in solitude where boulders lie.
Fogged in, you float and hear an egret's call.
A blurry light seeps from a muted sky.
Warblers carouse and make a tiny squall.
Fall's coinage scatters on the ancient duff.
The axe ascends and splits the maple grain.
Crags loom like anvils. Subtle wind's enough
to bless the moss, the dogwood's careful pain.
Dense drooping balsams mute the chainsaw's drone,
a growl in pungent air. This too shall pass.
Nothing you do can make you less alone.
The hill's no carpet, lake no sheet of glass.
Wait. Snow will cover all that's strange,
the waning moon cast down its gentle change.

The Mushroom Collector

She returns just as a worried moon
clears the hemlocks. You hear feet
on the path before seeing her emerge
in bleak light. The pouch at her side
bulges with mushrooms. Inside,
the smell of rampant growth gathers.
She tells you, "I love how they sponge out
overnight, spore-laden."

You sit at a table strewn with fans
and phalluses. Eyelash Cups, small red disks
ringed with fine hairs, cling to maple bark.
Dead Man's Fingers grow, it is said,
where bodies have fallen.
Amber Jelly Mushrooms rise from stumps.
You rub the skin of the Strangulated
Amanita as, outside, heavy mist blows in.
A loon calls the name of a cloud.

Now she pulls apart a Witch's Cap,
pausing over its leathery surface,
the stem's inner sinews.
She shows you how the Graceful Bolete
turns blue the moment you break it,
and how the gills of a Salmon
Unicorn Entoloma open, gentle
pink tinge hinting at flamingo
or the dust of Wyoming sunsets.
Out of a clump of moss the Yellow Coral,
clavaria pulchra, spreads oceanic fingers.

She assures you its flavor is safe.
You nibble, half hoping you'll explode
with growth like Alice, but nothing changes.
Well past the dinner hour, your appetite's gone.
Neither of you speaks for a long time.
You listen for mushrooms blooming through earth.

Under Gemini

The sun has dipped beyond the hill
across the lake. I'm on the dock waiting for stars
to surface, waiting as the sun gives way.
In the cabin up the trail a black stove's fire
sinks to ember. My wife and daughters turn
in early sleep, turn while kitchen coals tick out.
Where there is one bright body there is order:
Venus, planet falling fast, holds the sky alone
before all others, then slips down into haze.
Where two bodies, there is symmetry: two daughters
tug their blankets as the fire dies, the stove cools.

Now the dragon uncurls between the dippers
as they circumscribe Polaris, as they come round
empty. Now the rowboat worries its tether at my feet,
pulling away as surely as the stars wheel out.
Ruffled waters blur the heavens; I look up
to see a sky crowded beyond symmetry.
Invisible Scorpius must be coiled
low and horizontal, behind hemlocks
to the east. The slightest wind breathes
across uncertain waters. Leo stretches
somewhere, hidden in the sun's old glow.

Above, the star-borne twins are bound
perpetually together, arcing in hopeful tandem.
From the dock's firm surface I can feel the boat
tugging the rope taut. Pegasus, heavenly
winging, follows the swan gliding south
in her nebulous wake of white down.

My family sleeps, as I drift out
over the heaving lake. Lying back
on the boat's damp floor, leaving the land
out of it this time, I settle myself
where even the tips of trees disappear.

The Woodpecker

Late in the afternoon, following a day
        of small victories and clear weather,
I'm on the screen porch reading a book.
        Just when it seems the plot is becoming
labored and mechanical, the leading lady
        does something so unexpected
and perfect that to reveal it
        would spoil the story.
I lean back in the wicker chair,
        bite into my crisp apple,
and pause, letting the novel's world
        take me in like an orphan.

Then, for the second time this spring,
        I hear a pileated woodpecker pounding
the loblolly in the back yard
        above the centipede crawl
of the awakening grass. Red cap bobbing
        like a buoy on rough water,
he jackhammers the bark, shreds it
        into a shower of splinters.
Large as a hawk, he grips the tree
        and works as though starving
for weevils or simply exuberant
        in the force of his pounding.

The cat in the grass crouches, hunched
        and awed with the terror
of that fiery topknot in its frenzy.
        His earthbound tail is limp

and untwitching, his muscles
 poised for scuttling away
in the face of such fury
 during this gradual season of green.
At the pond down the road,
 a turtle balances on a log.
A heron patrols
 the shallows.

And now, lost in the season's goodness,
 I am struggling to fathom
how so quickly my thoughts retreat
 to the pond, the dark water,
the solitary turtle and heron
 in their oblivion,
how in a flash as brisk as the woodpecker's
 punishing rhythm I find myself
a century away from the novel's intrigue,
 thrust out of the captivation
I am so startled to leave and even now
 mourn as it sinks from view.

Gold Country

Time to rake aside the winter medicine
of oak leaf in the garden.
beneath it all, the swollen earth.
Sunflower stalks rattle in the wind,
ten months after seed. Stones percolate
up through the ground. I lug them off,

then open the whole globe with my shovel.
I tuck in tomato plants,
expectant as ova. In shallow troughs
I sew zinnia seed. In the sanctuary
of July their red hues will rise
from clotted soil that reaches China.

While I plant, I hear the chanteuse,
gravelly voice and sequins spangling
the composted air. Her song says
steal away at sundown, lean
the implements of culture against a tree,
and hasten to town.

Nature, said Heraclitus, likes to hide
herself. I could wash and wash
these soiled knuckles and still
they'd be my father's
with his country bearing.
Minutes away I drink in Sacramento.

Dark loam coats my boot heels.
In the Golden Acorn Tavern
a saxophone drains even the blood
of beets. The singer waits, toying
with glass beads, and gives
me the eye, alert for her next cue.

Elegy for Unfinished Poems

A cube of bricks, askew
in an otherwise empty field
awaits the mason
who could fashion a foundation.
What's weathered seasons begins
to sink as Queen Anne's lace
rises around it.

Here, the cars of Cuba
roam their wrinkled page.
One fisherman's jitney
sputters, rods jutting
from smudged windows,
sinkers and hooks clinking
toward the bay.

The rusty hulks stall
in the page's frame, lost ancestors.
One patriarch, right arm behind his back,
freezes grimly for the photographer.
His broad left hand, all knuckles,
hangs beside a watch chain he may have
borrowed for this sepia study.

The uncle who died just last fall
once had a trick wooden box.
It slid open to reveal
a nickel-sized slot.
Drop in a coin, shut the tiny drawer,
and it was gone, only to reappear
if you swiveled the box around.

This shard of text,
like the bricks, the cars,
the patriarch, haunts me like
an old lover's face. I return to it
as the tongue returns to the chipped tooth,
as the mother ponders the wayward child
in the blurred ink of night.

Circulation

Every poem struggles not to be
about itself, as it ravels words
like balled yarn looping back
to find an origin, a foothold,
an opening, a point of departure
for nowhere special but somewhere
different. Notice this time
it's a shade of blue hovering
between a computer's electric
glow and the washed vacancy of indigo.
No sooner does that long line,
its period, its color evoking
flat plantations, hint at closure,
than comes another line over
the matted globe, drops a spaghetti-
thin shadow and settles against all
the rest, turning the whole deeper
and more cerulean, spun in the ocean's
lap or cut from a hank of sky.
Now the effect's rectangular,
more cleared plot than stranded ball.
It yearns for elsewhere, the way
a plowed field ends at the tree line
but transports you like a carpet
to more open land, a stand
of corn two weeks further along
than yours or a field of alfalfa
ripe for mowing. You see how blue
has wrapped its way to green,
how sickled green makes golden hay.

The growth becomes a journey
to Rumpelstiltskin, his name a woman's
salvation. She left the knuckle-numbing
straw forever, abandoned her wheel abruptly
as St. Joan, whom saints beckoned
into battle. We are left
with a threadbare tale, snarls of metaphor,
and fire rising like hot words
into a sky colored some blue
that didn't exist before we started
and will never come down again.

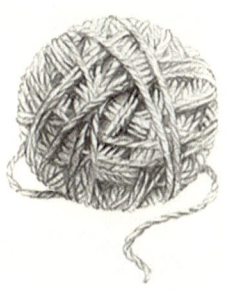

ABOUT THE AUTHOR

 KEN AUTREY lives in Auburn, Alabama, where he helps coordinate the Third Thursday Poetry Series. He earned degrees from Davidson College, Auburn University, and the University of South Carolina. He is an Emeritus Professor of English at Francis Marion University in South Carolina, where he taught poetry, creative nonfiction, and advanced composition. Previously, he served as a Peace Corps Volunteer in Ghana and taught at Tougaloo College in Mississippi. He spent one year as a visiting professor at Hiroshima University in Japan. Autrey's work has appeared in *Chattahoochee Review, Cimarron Review, Poetry Northwest, Southern Poetry Review, Texas Review* and many other journals. He has published four chapbooks: *Pilgrims* (Main Street Rag), *Rope Lesson* (Longleaf Press), *The Wake of the Year* (Solomon and George Press), and *Penelope in Repose* (Evening Street Press). He is married to Janne Debes. They have two daughters and six grandchildren.

Author photograph by Janne Debes

ACKNOWLEDGEMENTS

Thanks to the editors of journals in which poems in this collection first appeared:

Alligator Juniper: "Still Life with Piranhas"
Birmingham Poetry Review: "Electricity," "The Invention of Time"
California Quarterly: "Christmas Cards"
Chattahoochee Review: "Heat Wave", "Expedition"
Cimarron Review: "Mask"
Comstock Review: "Pilgrims"
Cumberland River Review: "What I Thought I Knew"
The Devil's Millhopper: "Under Gemini"
Embers: "The Mushroom Collector"
Emrys Journal: "Lighthouse," "Rope Lesson"
Hubbub: "Gold Country"
King Log: "On My 52nd Birthday"
Levee: "Kayak"
Lullwater Review: "Elegy for Unfinished Poems"
Phase and Cycle: "Mnemonist "
Poem: "Home Port," "My Daughter Rowing,"
Poetry Northwest: "Circulation," "Eclipse," "Sahel"
South Carolina Review: "Altar," Part 1 of "Gravity" (entitled
        "Baggage")
Southern Poetry Review: "Hilyer's Junkyard"
Southern Quarterly: "The Woodpecker"
Tar River Poetry: "Elegy for My Father," "The Explosion of the
        Kopper Kettle"

Thanks also to the editors of anthologies and chapbooks in which some of these poems were first published or reprinted:

"Before the Wedding" and "School Lunchroom" are included in *The Southern Poetry Anthology, Volume I: South Carolina*. Eds. Stephen Gardner and William Wright. Texas Review Press, 2007.

"Circulation," "Gold Country," "The Mushroom Collector," "Pilgrims," and "Sahel" appear in *Pilgrims*, a chapbook published by Main Street Rag, 2010.

"Elegy for My Father," "Gravity," "Hilyer's Junkyard," "*In Medias Res*," "Mints," "Mnemonist," "Rope Lesson," and "Shotguns" appear in *Rope Lesson*, a chapbook published by Longleaf Press, 2013.

"The Ice Skaters" appears in *You, Year.* Ed. Tom Johnson. Harbinger Publications, 1996.

"*In Medias Res*" was selected by Dan Albergotti for first prize in the South Carolina Poetry Initiative Annual Contest, 2011.

"Rope Lesson," "Shotguns," and "Talking to My Granddaughter" are included in *A Millennial Sampler of South Carolina Poetry.* Eds. Gilbert Allen and William E. Rogers. Ninety-Six Press, 2005.

"Under Gemini" appears in *From the Green Horseshoe: Poems by James Dickey's Students.* University of South Carolina Press, 1987.

For the full Dos Madres Press catalog:
www.dosmadres.com

www.ingramcontent.com/pod-product-compliance
Lightning Source LLC
Chambersburg PA
CBHW031218120626
46545CB00003B/895